CRIME
Solvers

# Murder FILE
## A Killer's Manual

## by Edward Nicholson

Consultant: Dr. John P. Cassella
Principal Lecturer in Forensic Science
Staffordshire University, England

BEARPORT
PUBLISHING

New York, New York

## Credits

Cover, © Matt Olsen/istockphoto.com, © Jennifer Sheets/istockphoto.com, © Christopher O Driscoll/istockphoto.com, and © Rex Features; Title Page, © Rex Features; 4, © PA Photos/Andrew Parsons/PA Archive; 5T, © Shutterstock; 5B, © Rex Features; 6T, © Ben Granville/Rex Features; 6B, © PA Photos/PA Archive; 7T, © Ben Dome/Rex Features; 7B, © Shutterstock; 8, © Mikael Karlsson/Arrestingimages.com; 9T, © Rex Features; 9B, © Charles Orrico/Superstock; 10, © Alex Woods/Rex Features; 11L, © Linda Shannon/ istockphoto; 11R, © Anglia Press Agency; 12, © Mikael Karlsson/Alamy; 13T, © Carmen Martínez Banús/istockphoto; 13B, © Don Smetzer/Alamy; 14T, © Shutterstock; 14B, © Shutterstock; 15, © Shutterstock; 16T, © Mikael Karlsson/Arrestingimages.com; 17T, © Shutterstock; 17B, © Shutterstock; 18T, © Arthur Turner/Alamy; 18B, © Shutterstock; 19T, © Shutterstock; 19B, © Stefan Klein/istockphoto; 20, © Shutterstock; 21T, © Shutterstock; 21B, © Steve Allen/Alamy; 22, © PA Photos/Andrew Parsons/PA Archive; 23, © Simon Rawles/Alamy; 24, © Priscilla Coleman/Rex Features; 25T, © brandXpictures; 25B, © David Playford/istockphoto; 26R, © Michael Donne/Science Photo Library; 28T, © Rex Features; 28B, © Shutterstock; 29, © Shutterstock; 30, © fStop/Superstock.

Every effort has been made by ticktock Entertainment Ltd. to trace copyright holders. We apologize in advance for any omissions. We would be pleased to insert the appropriate acknowledgments in any subsequent edition of this publication.

Publisher: Kenn Goin
Editorial Director: Adam Siegel
Project Editor: Dinah Dunn
Creative Director: Spencer Brinker
Original Design: ticktock Entertainment Ltd.

*Library of Congress Cataloging-in-Publication Data*

Nicholson, Edward.
 Murder file : a killer's manual / by Edward Nicholson.
    p. cm. — (Crime solvers)
 Includes bibliographical references and index.
 ISBN-13: 978-1-59716-549-5 (lib. bdg.)
 ISBN-10: 1-59716-549-2 (lib. bdg.)
1. Mendel, Anne, d. 2005—Juvenile literature. 2. Adeyoola, Kemi—Juvenile literature. 3. Murder—Investigation—England—London—Case studies—Juvenile literature. 4. Murder—England—London—Case studies—Juvenile literature. 5. Juvenile homicide—England—London—Case studies—Juvenile literature. 6. Evidence, Criminal—England—London—Juvenile literature. I. Title.

HV8079.H6N53 2008
364.152'3092—dc22

                              2007020227

# Contents

# A Terrible Sight

**M**arch 14, 2005 seemed like an ordinary day for Leonard and Anne Mendel. The retired couple was living peacefully in a suburb of London. Leonard left their home in the morning to run some errands. Anne stayed behind because she wasn't feeling well.

The Mendel's neighborhood in Golders Green

Leonard returned home a few hours later to a terrible sight. At the bottom of the stairs, Leonard found his wife, Anne, lying in a pile of clothes. "I didn't know if she was alive or dead." Leonard said. "At that time I didn't notice one of the walls was covered with blood."

Leonard tried to call for an ambulance. The phone didn't work. Whoever had hurt Anne had also cut the phone line in the hall.

The phone line in the hall had been cut.

## FACT FILE

### Case Notes

**The victim:**
Anne Mendel, 84, wife of Leonard Mendel, 81

**Cause of death:**
14 stab wounds

**Crime scene:**
Golders Green, London, England

**Date of murder:**
March 14, 2005

Anne Mendel

5

# A Killer on the Loose

Luckily, the phone in the kitchen still worked. Leonard Mendel used it to call for an ambulance. While he waited for it to arrive, he frantically tried to **revive** his wife. It was no use, however.

Anne Mendel was pronounced dead at 12:45 P.M. She had been stabbed 14 times. Her body was taken for an autopsy.

Leonard Mendel

Police in front of Anne Mendel's house in Golders Green

Investigators were concerned. The violent crime suggested a dangerous killer was on the loose. They carefully searched the crime scene for **clues**. The front-door lock had not been forced open. Anne might have known her attacker and let the killer inside.

The police released details of the murder to the press. They hoped someone would come forward with information before anyone else was hurt.

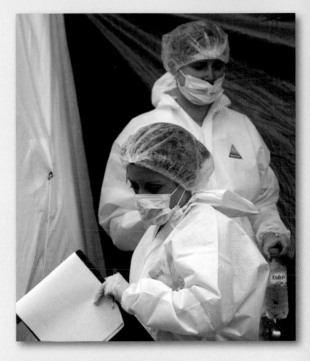

Crime-scene investigators search for evidence.

During an autopsy, a body is examined for injuries and evidence.

# Cause of Death

**A** forensic pathologist performed an autopsy on Anne Mendel's body. It was determined that she had died from her stab wounds. The pathologist carefully examined Anne's body to find any **evidence** left by the killer.

A small sample of **DNA** was found under Anne's fingernail. This sample was checked against a **database** of the DNA of known criminals.

When a murder victim scratches his or her attacker, DNA evidence from skin cells may be trapped under the victim's fingernails.

Police were hoping a match would lead them to a **suspect**. It did. The DNA belonged to an 18-year-old girl named Kemi Adeyoola.

Murder suspect Kemi Adeyoola

## FACT FILE

## DNA Testing

The recent science of DNA testing has increased investigators' chances of finding a criminal.

- DNA is short for deoxyribonucleic acid. People carry unique DNA combinations in their cells.

- The police keep a database of the DNA of known criminals.

- In a murder case, forensic scientists compare samples of DNA they find on the victim with those the police have on file. This was how they found Kemi Adeyoola.

A scientist prepares a DNA sample for testing.

# The Prime Suspect

Kemi Adeyoola did not seem like someone who would commit murder. She was the teenage daughter of millionaire businessman and former boxer, Bola Adeyoola. He was divorced from Kemi's mother, Mercuria.

Adeyoola had gotten into trouble in the past. She was kicked out of boarding school. She then moved in with her mother in Golders Green in north London. For almost a year, they lived next door to Anne and Leonard Mendel.

Anne Mendel's home in Golders Green

During this time, Kemi began **shoplifting**. After getting caught a number of times, Adeyoola was sent to Bullwood Hall prison. A sample of her DNA was put into the police database. She served three months of a six-month **sentence**. Adeyoola was released a few months before Anne Mendel was killed.

## FACT FILE

### An Unlikely Suspect

Kemi Adeyoola was only 16 years old when she went to prison for shoplifting.

- "It was the first time I had truly been placed away from my family against my will," Adeyoola said.

- Only about 80 young women between the ages of 15 and 17 are imprisoned in England and Wales, compared to 2,700 young men.

Shoplifting is the most common crime among young women in England.

Bullwood Hall prison

# The Arrest

On May 12, 2005, Adeyoola was arrested for killing Anne Mendel. Police told her that her DNA had been found at the crime scene. They asked her how it had gotten there.

Adeyoola said that on March 13, the day before the murder, she went to Sally Beauty Supply in Golders Green to buy two hair-relaxing kits. She saw Anne Mendel on the corner of Golders Green Road. Adeyoola said she offered Anne her hand to help her cross the street.

Kemi Adeyoola was living with her younger sister, Sade, in Belsize Park when she was arrested.

As they walked, Adeyoola said Anne stumbled. "She must have caught her foot on some gravel or something," she said. As Anne slipped, Adeyoola said Anne scratched her hand. The police didn't believe her story.

Adeyoola claimed she helped Anne Mendel cross the street.

## FACT FILE

### Adeyoola's Lies

When police looked into Kemi Adeyoola's story, they knew she was lying.

- A search of Adeyoola's apartment showed that she owned no hair-relaxing kits.

- Sally Beauty Supply does not sell the type of kits Adeyoola said she bought there.

Sally Beauty Supply

# Lies, Lies, and More Lies

**P**olice looked deeper into Adeyoola's story. They checked her cell phone records. The records showed that on March 13, Adeyoola was not in Golders Green, helping Anne Mendel cross the street. Her calls placed her in central London.

Adeyoola also claimed that on the morning of the murder, March 14, she was at a bus garage in northwest London. She said she went there to get a purse she had left on a bus.

Adeyoola claimed she was at a bus garage the morning of the murder.

However, calls made from Adeyoola's phone at 11:24 A.M. on the morning of the murder told a different story. Those calls placed her near her home in Belsize Park. Police suspected she had made those calls after returning home from killing Anne Mendel.

Police tracked Adeyoola through her cell phone records.

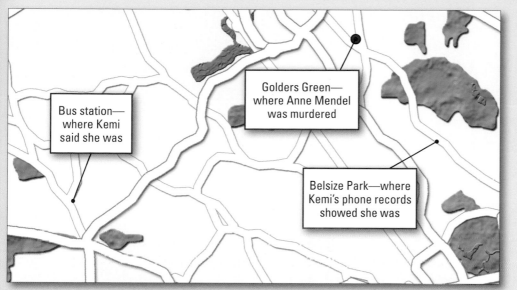

Bus station—where Kemi said she was

Golders Green—where Anne Mendel was murdered

Belsize Park—where Kemi's phone records showed she was

This map of London shows where Kemi Adeyoola claimed to be when the murder took place.

# FACT FILE

## Cell Phone Records

Police can track suspected criminals through their use of cell phones.

- Cell phones do not record exactly where they were used. However, calls are sent through base stations. Police can find out which base station a person was near when he or she placed a call. They use that information to figure out a caller's location at the time of a crime.

- Some information in phones cannot be permanently erased. For example, if a criminal has deleted text messages, the phone company will still have a record of them.

By reviewing Adeyoola's phone records, police were able to determine that she was lying about where she was on the day of the murder.

A cell phone base station

# A Surprising Discovery

**A**fter some investigation, the police discovered something surprising about Adeyoola. When she had been in prison for shoplifting, guards had searched her cell. They had found a murder **manual** Adeyoola had written. It was called *Prison and After: Making Life Count*. This 18-page book described how to murder an old woman and take her money.

Prison cells are often searched to make sure prisoners aren't hiding anything.

At the time it was discovered, Adeyoola said it was merely a crime novel she was writing. She said, "I'd been reading crime thriller books. . . . and it fascinated me and I thought I'd give it a go."

Adeyoola claimed the murder manual was just "the scribblings of a 16-year-old girl."

## FACT FILE

### Fact or Fiction?

In Adeyoola's murder manual, she described how to attack an elderly woman in a wealthy area.

- "Run lightly and silently behind her and cover her mouth with a gloved hand," she wrote.

- "Make her so scared she cooperates. Keep calm, composed, and silent. She must cooperate or take a knife to her throat. Tell her, 'this is your only warning.'"

Adeyoola planned to follow a rich, elderly victim home.

# The Murder Manual

In Adeyoola's murder manual, she described in detail the weapons and equipment needed to successfully murder someone. These included knives, handcuffs, and **stun guns**. Adeyoola wrote about buying drugs that cause memory loss and **paralysis** in the victim. She also explained how she'd disguise herself in a long, black wig and a fat suit so she wouldn't be recognized.

A stun gun uses electricity to hurt people without killing them.

Adeyoola planned to buy weapons to terrify her helpless victim.

Adeyoola planned what she would do once she had forced her way into her victim's home. She would order the woman to turn off any alarm and to check if anyone was home. Then Adeyoola would gag and blindfold the woman and handcuff her to a radiator. She then went into gruesome detail how she would kill the woman and get rid of her body.

## FACT FILE
### Fooled Again

While Adeyoola was in prison for shoplifting, she worked with **psychologist** Lydia Sear. The report of their conversations proved that Adeyoola was a skilled liar.

- Adeyoola pretended that she had received "A"s in school. This lie led Sear to report that Adeyoola could do well if released from prison.

- The psychologist also said Adeyoola was unlikely ever to commit violence.

Adeyoola lied about her grades in school.

# A Trial Run

**A**deyoola's plan was to not only murder a weak old woman but to also steal her money. In her manual, she described how she would torture her victim into revealing her private bank-security numbers and the code to her **safe**.

Adeyoola had hoped to make as much as $6 million with her plan. She even described how she would spend the money.

Many older people keep their money and valuables in safes in their homes.

Yet Anne Mendel was not wealthy. Why had Adeyoola killed her?

One of the lawyers working on the case argued that the murder of Anne Mendel was a "trial run." Adeyoola was testing her plan. If it worked, she would then murder someone wealthy. Clearly, Adeyoola did not expect to be caught.

Adeyoola planned to wear gloves so she wouldn't leave any fingerprints.

## FACT FILE

### A Psychopath

Many people investigating the Kemi Adeyoola case considered her to be a **psychopath**. Detective Inspector Steve Morris said the murder showed "an unusual level of violence in a girl so young."

- A psychopath is a person who cannot share or understand the feelings of others. Adeyoola did not seem to care about the pain she caused the Mendel family.

- Psychopaths are very good liars. Adeyoola boasted that she had been able to trick a social worker into feeling sorry for her during an interview. She did this by crying and mumbling.

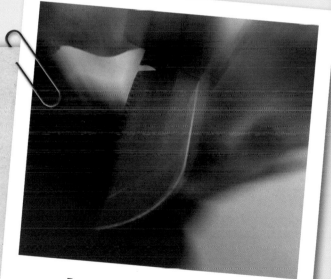

Psychopaths don't feel bad when they hurt others.

# False Alibi

The police charged Adeyoola with the murder of Anne Mendel. She was sent to Holloway Prison in north London until her **trial**. While in prison, Adeyoola began to plot with her sister Sade how to create a fake **alibi** for the time of the murder.

The sisters placed an ad in a newspaper. In it, they asked anyone who had seen Kemi Adeyoola on a bus the morning of the murder to contact her lawyers. If someone came forward, Adeyoola would have an alibi.

Holloway Prison

Adeyoola then approached another prisoner, Natasha Greenwood. Could she find a person who would agree to be paid to say he or she had seen Adeyoola on a bus at the time of the murder? Greenwood pretended to agree. Instead, she told police about Adeyoola's plot.

Holloway is Europe's largest women's prison.

# The Court Case

**K**emi Adeyoola's trial began at London's Old Bailey courthouse on June 6, 2006. She tried to gain sympathy from the judge and jury by crying and shaking in court when she was questioned. After hearing the case, the **jury** took 23 hours to reach a decision.

On June 27, 2006, Adeyoola was found guilty of the murder of Anne Mendel. She was also found guilty of trying to trick the court by creating a false alibi.

This illustration shows Kemi Adeyoola being questioned. Cameras are not allowed in British courts.

Judge Richard Hone called her a "cold-blooded killer and a serious and continuing danger to the public." He said, "I think you actually wanted to experience what it felt like killing somebody in cold blood, possibly to write about it but more probably to boast about it, and possibly even do it again." The following day, Adeyoola was sentenced to life in prison.

Adeyoola will be behind bars until at least 2026.

The statue of Justice on top of the Old Bailey courthouse

## FACT FILE

### Adeyoola's Family

- Kemi Adeyoola's younger sister, Sade, was sentenced to two years in jail for plotting to create a fake alibi.

- Adeyoola's father, Bola, described his daughter as a "monster." He said, "What she did was evil. She is no longer my daughter."

# Case Closed

## March 14, 2005

Anne Mendel is brutally stabbed to death in her home.

## May 12, 2005

Kemi Adeyoola is arrested for murder after police find a match between her DNA and the DNA on Anne Mendel's hand.

## May 2005–November 2005

The police discover that, while Kemi Adeyoola was in prison, she had written a murder manual. In this book, she describes how she would kill an old woman.

## December 2005

While awaiting trial, Adeyoola tries to hire someone to lie and provide her with a fake alibi. She is caught when another prisoner tells police of the plot.

## June 6, 2006

The trial of Kemi Adeyoola begins in London.

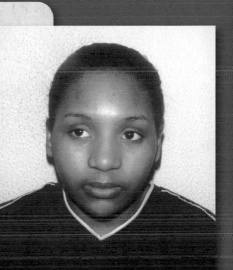

## June 27, 2006

Kemi Adeyoola is found guilty of the murder of Anne Mendel and of trying to trick the court.

## June 28, 2006

Kemi Adeyoola is sentenced to life in prison.

# Crime Solving Up Close

## DNA Matching

A DNA sample found on the body of Anne Mendel was enough to lead police to her killer, Kemi Adeyoola.

- DNA is a unique chemical code people carry in the cells of their bodies. People get their DNA from their parents.

- Scientists only need a tiny amount of DNA, which can be found in a drop of blood or a single eyelash, to create a DNA profile.

- When people are arrested, the inside of their mouths are wiped with a cotton swab. This gives the police a sample of their DNA.

- When the police have a DNA profile from a crime scene, they compare it to a computer database. This contains the DNA profiles of millions of criminals.

A forensic scientist studies a DNA profile.

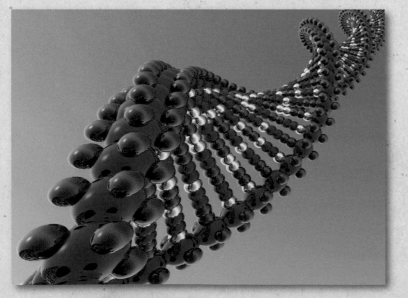

This computer model shows the shape of a DNA molecule.

# Documentary Evidence

The murder manual written by Kemi Adeyoola was one of the main pieces of evidence used against her.

- Documents that are used as evidence in a trial are known as documentary evidence. They are usually written or typed documents, but they can involve other forms, such as film.

Examples of documentary evidence include:

- Photographs
- Official documents
- Letters
- Films
- Tape recordings
- Printed E-mails

Letters often contain important documentary evidence.

# Crime Solving Up Close

## Autopsy

When police need to know how someone died, they will ask a forensic pathologist to do an autopsy. Pathologists look for clues on a body to find out the cause of death. The pathologist who examined Anne Mendel's body found DNA from Kemi Adeyoola. Here are some of the steps pathologists follow when doing an autopsy.

- The body is laid out on a table and thoroughly examined for injuries.

- The forensic pathologist makes a cut from behind the ear to the top of the leg to open up the body.

- The organs, including the stomach, lungs, and heart, are taken out and examined.

- Samples from the body are sent to a **toxicology** lab for testing. This is especially important if police think the person may have been poisoned. The lab checks to see if unusual drugs or poisons are in the body.

- The organs are then returned to the body and it is sewn up. The body is buried.

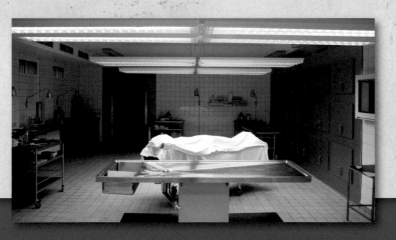

An autopsy room

# Glossary

**alibi** (AL-ih-*bye*) a claim by a person accused of a crime that he or she was somewhere else when the crime was committed

**clues** (KLOOZ) objects or information that make it easier for a person to solve a mystery

**database** (DAY-tuh-bayss) information stored in a computer

**DNA** (DEE EN AY) the molecule that carries the genetic code for a living thing

**evidence** (EV-uh-duhnss) objects or information that can be used to prove whether something is true

**forensic pathologists** (fuh-REN-sik path-OL-uh-jists) doctors who study dead bodies to find out the cause of death

**jury** (JU-ree) a group of people that listens to facts at a trial and makes a decision about who is to blame

**manual** (MAN-yoo-uhl) a book that tells a person how to do something

**paralysis** (puh-RAL-uh-siss) the inability to move or feel a part of one's body

**psychologist** (sye-KOL-us-jist) a person who studies people's minds and the way they behave

**psychopath** (SYE-kuh-*path*) a person who is mentally ill

**revive** (ri-VIVE) bring someone back to consciousness after he or she has been unconscious

**safe** (SAYF) a strong box for locking away valuables

**sentence** (SEN-tuhnss) the amount of time a guilty person must serve in jail as punishment for a crime

**shoplifting** (SHOP-lift-ing) stealing something from a store

**stun guns** (STUHN GUHNS) weapons that use electricity to hurt without killing

**suspect** (SUHSS-pekt) a person who is thought to have committed a crime

**toxicology** (*toks*-us-KOL-uh-jee) the study of the effect of poisonous substances on the body

**trial** (TRYE-uhl) an examination of evidence in a court of law to decide if a charge is true

# Index

# Read More

**Hunter, William**. *Mark and Trace Analysis.* Broomall, PA: Mason Crest Publishers (2005).

**Platt, Richard**. *Forensics.* Boston, MA: Houghton Mifflin Company (2005).

**Twist, Clint, and Denis Kilcommons**. *The Great Forensic Challenge.* Hauppauge, NY: Barron's Educational Series, Incorporated (2005).

# Learn More Online

To learn more about crime solving and the Murder Manual case, visit
**www.bearportpublishing.com/CrimeSolvers**

# About the Author

Edward Nicholson is a freelance journalist and writer
who lives in London. His nonfiction has appeared in papers and magazines
including the *Telegraph*, the *Observer*, and the *Guardian*.